"From a low-earning playwright's troubles to reflections on why the Palestinians are justified in their resentment of Israel. Wallace Shawn: Fearless!"

—*GQ*, Best Books of 2009

"Full of what you might call conversation starters: tricky propositions about morality . . . politics, privilege, runaway nationalist fantasies, collective guilt and art as a force for change (or not). It's a treat to hear [Shawn] speak his curious mind."

—*O*, *The Oprah Magazine*

"Wallace Shawn's career as a playwright has been uncompromisingly devoted to proving, again and again, that theater is an ideal medium for exploring difficult matters of great consequence. The qualities that make his dramatic work so challenging, startling, unsettling, sensual, mind-and-soul expanding, so indispensable, are equally in evidence in the marvelous political and theatrical essays collected here. The basic faith of politically progressive people, that human beings are full of decent impulses perverted by political and economic malevolence, is in Shawn's writing held up to the liveliest, sharpest scrutiny imaginable; not, as in so much reactionary art, to shift blame from oppressor to oppressed, or from artifice to Nature, not to insist that we're innately, inescapably incapable of change, but rather as a scrupulous accounting of the slippery ethics, dream logic, fear-ridden resistance to progress, disturbing desires, of the greatest problem confronting all our hopes for a better, transformed world: Us, the actors in our collective drama. His essays are without sentiment and entirely resistant to the easy comforts of despair. Complexities are rendered delightfully plain, obfuscations are unsnarled and illuminated, clarity and rational thought are organized to plumb mysteries, and mysteries are respected and celebrated. Shawn's language, his unmistakable, original voice, felicitous, is unadorned, elegant, immediate, true. He's also a brilliant interviewer, as everyone who's seen *My Dinner with André* (which is just about everyone) knows. And, of course, he's very funny."

—Tony Kushner

"Wallace Shawn is a bracing antidote to the op-ed dreariness of political and artistic journalism in the West. He takes you back to the days when intellectuals had the wit and concentration to formulate great questions—and to make the reader want to answer them."

—David Hare

NIGHT THOUGHTS

An Essay

Wallace Shawn

Haymarket Books
Chicago, IL

Published by
Haymarket Books
P.O. Box 180165
Chicago, IL 60618
773-583-7884
info@haymarketbooks.org / www.haymarketbooks.org

ISBN: 978-1-64259-374-7

Trade distribution:
In the US through Consortium Book Sales and Distribution,
www.cbsd.com
In the UK, Turnaround Publisher Services, www.turnaround-uk.com
In Canada, Publishers Group Canada, www.pgcbooks.ca
All other countries, Ingram Publisher Services International,
intlsales@perseusbooks.com

This book was published with the generous support
of the Wallace Action Fund and Lannan Foundation.

The text and display of this book are composed in Kepler Standard.

Cover design by Rachel Cohen. Cover photography by Tim Knox.

Printed in Canada by union labor.

Library of Congress CIP Data is available.

10 9 8 7 6 5 4 3 2 1

Murder

Night. A hotel. A dark room on a high floor. Outside the hotel, miles of empty city streets, silent, gray, like gray fields in winter. Inside, I'm alone in a very cold room with a buzzing minibar. Through the window, far below in the street, I can see a couple of thin, solitary, wandering men, one with a hat cocked at a debonair angle. Then I turn on a dim lamp and stare at the newspaper, and my eye goes as always to the stories about crime, the murders. A crime of passion—jealousy, frenzy—a body falling in the shower. Strange deaths in a quiet suburb—an odd weapon—a serial killer? My senses quicken, my lethargy falls away. They're writing about me. Well, no, not me, not quite, not yet. But I know, as I read, that I'm not reading as the victim, I'm reading as the murderer.

* * *

In a courtroom, the case of a robbery gone wrong. The thief had been inside the house when the man who owned it unexpectedly came home. The thief had gone after the man with a knife, and when he was asked, "Why did you stab him thirty-eight times when you knew he was dead after the first blow?" the murderer's answer was, "I don't know." Murderers always seem to say, "I don't know"—unless they say, "I can't remember what happened."

* * *

Then, on the television, a different kind of murder. Brightly dressed university students in pools of blood, their books scattered all over the street. The Islamic State. A machine gun. Screaming. Sobbing. An Arab empire in the fourteenth century?

* * *

The hotel itself, in this dead, ruined neighborhood—all shards and scraps floating in the wind—is rather magnificent, resplendent with ballrooms, as if we were living in the nineteenth century. Not long before, some young people from a housing project in the neighborhood had put together quite a lot of money in order to dress up in tuxedos and evening gowns and hold a celebration in one of the ballrooms. As the party wore on, one boy thought another boy had flirted with his date. A fight broke out. Mayhem in the ballroom. Then shots were fired, and the party ended in bondage and death—one boy gone forever, another boy handcuffed and carried away.

Night

The television screen keeps turning back obsessively, crazily, to the face of Trump. Oh my God—will this never end? I turn off the television, turn out the light. When I try to fall asleep, Trump keeps jumping back at me, then he slowly fades out, and I think about myself, the course of my life. Words and thoughts from the ancestors—my parents, their friends, the authors of books written long ago—begin to come to me. They repeat and repeat, as if of their own accord.

Words, thoughts, names, phrases—sometimes images as well. My childhood is very, very close. A frighteningly thin wispy-haired man in a gray suit holding a long cigarette standing by a window that's crackling with reflections—he's talking forcefully—it's all about Beethoven . . .

Good luck from the beginning. People were paid to take care of me. We lived in a large apartment building in a very big city, and if my mother wanted something heavy to be moved from one room to another, or if she thought the dishwasher was making a peculiar sound, she would call the building superintendent, and someone would appear to fix the problem. Books and music from the very beginning.

Books and music. Nobody ever exactly said this to me, but I took it as implied: what I was going to do in the life ahead of me was to try to be happy.

That was going to be my principal professional responsibility. I would wake up every day and try to become happier.

For various reasons, my friends and I all turned out to be, to varying degrees, what people decades ago used to call "downward mobile." Our positions in society are somewhat lower than the ones our parents held. During the years when I was growing up, my father never went to a grocery store to buy food. Other people did that for him. He never walked home from the grocery store carrying a bag of groceries. He never walked up flights of stairs to his apartment while carrying his groceries. I do those things. I live in a small building, and if there's a problem with the electricity or the plumbing, I can't ask a building superintendent to send someone over to fix it. All the same, my luck has held. I live in a quiet, tranquil part of town. I write. I read. I visit friends. I go to concerts. I go to restaurants.

When I was twenty, I learned about the lives people led in the imperial Japanese court in the eleventh century. It was all described in the novel *The Tale of Genji* by Lady Murasaki Shikibu and *The Pillow Book* of Sei Shōnagon, which was a sort of diary or journal. I could tell right away that this was for me—women and men who had nothing to do all day but speculate and talk about love and beauty. Or so it seemed. Reclining on pillows next to each other, they wrote letters and poems from early in the morning till late at night, on perfumed paper of many different colors. It seemed like a life to aspire to, anyway.

Anxieties

Obviously I'm upset about what my species has turned out to be—the species that went mad and destroyed the planet. It's unbelievable to recall how respected and admired the human animal was at one time. It's as if the old family dog, once universally beloved, had suddenly become rabid, his muzzle now covered with foam, his presence terrifying. And of course I'm upset about—why should I deny it?—I'm very upset about the Islamic State, about all the various successors of Osama bin Laden, and all the successors of the successors, the crazy bin Ladenists, now themselves splitting into hostile factions. I'm frightened of all the things they might decide to do, the dirty bombs, the poison gas. Sometimes I wonder, did this individual person, bin Laden, really have anything to do with planning the attacks of that horrible day in 2001? Who knows? Most of the evidence they talk about seems to come from people who were tortured—how can you believe it? But everyone agrees that bin Laden was pleased about what happened on that day. Anyway, we made him the symbol of it. Someone had to be. And so he had to be killed, obviously. Now his followers are stronger than ever, and it's awful, it's sickening, to know that there are these people out there in the world who would like to hurt me, who would like to eliminate me, whether they're standing next to me in the line at the airport or plotting secretly in a desert in Yemen. It's a terrible thought.

I'm also upset about "morality," not a word you hear much in conversation, really, but both my parents and my teachers in school were great devotees of it. They loved morality. I sometimes ask myself, What strange demon would have created an animal that could say to itself, "I'm doing this, and I want to do it, and I'm glad I'm doing it, but I shouldn't be doing it, because it's not 'right,' it's 'wrong.'" It's so peculiar. "Right" and "wrong" were like two little chimes that were constantly being struck in my parents' apartment. And as I go about my life, the chimes are still being struck inside my head, and I sometimes wonder—chime—if something about the way I live—chime—might somehow be "wrong"—chime chime.

Civilization

When I was in my late twenties, I visited a small, dark apartment in a bohemian section of town, and it was much rougher than the apartments my friends and I had grown up in. The tiny sink in the bathroom looked like it hadn't even been installed by a professional plumber. I was frightened by the smallness and the darkness of the apartment, and when I first walked into it I felt very ill at ease, but after a while the place began to seem rather warm and cozy, and I started to feel quite comfortable there, perhaps more comfortable than I'd ever felt in any other place, because I was drawn to the mysterious, alluring woman who lived in the apartment. She apparently didn't mind that the apartment was so small and dark—she seemed to think it wasn't really that bad. She could read there. She could even cook there—and she cooked quite a number of very delicious things. She could listen to music there—she had quite a few records—but at a certain moment she shocked me by saying that she thought civilization might have been a mistake, a mistake from the beginning. Excuse me?—my God—that was such an unsettling thing to say. It really disturbed me. I got very upset and couldn't understand what in the world she meant. Civilization? Civilization could only be good, from my point of view. Without civilization—well—all the things I cared about—and actually, all the things she seemed to care about too—they wouldn't have existed—no books, no music, no bohemian section of the city, no city at all. She'd come to the city to find a kind of freedom that couldn't have existed without civilization. Even the relationship we were about to embark on couldn't have existed without civilization.

And I could still remember the vivid images that had formed in my mind when I was a very young boy, and one of my teachers had spoken of the magnificent loam that had been created when the Nile overflowed its banks. So much that was glorious had grown out of the fertility of that extraordinary loam—pyramids, paintings, astonishing sculptures. . . . And I remembered the phrase, "Civilization means specialization." The brilliant idea that the sandal-maker wouldn't need to grow food, because he could get his food from the farmer in exchange for sandals, and the pharaoh didn't need to grow food or make sandals because the farmer and the sandal-maker paid taxes to the pharaoh so he could buy food and sandals and even hire painters and sculptors to create paintings and scultures. Incredibly clever. And I remembered that that frighteningly thin old wispy-haired man had said, in that room full of ashtrays and whiskey, something to the effect that all of civilization was justified by the fact that it finally produced Beethoven, the beauty of whose work was a kind of absolute—unanswerable and undeniable. And yet what the woman in the apartment had said stayed with me for weeks, then for years. It stayed with me and upset me, and I kept thinking about it. And about two decades later she stood beside me in a square in East Berlin as we read Brecht's poem carved in stone:

Wer baute das sieben-törige Theben?
In den Büchen stehen die Namen von
    Königen.
Haben die Königen die Felsenbrocken
    herbeigeschleppt? . . .

11

Who built Thebes with its seven gates?
In books, we're given the names of kings.
Did the kings carry on their own backs
    those massive fragments of stone? . . .

In his sixteen-line poem, Brecht quarreled with "the books." "The books" talked about the kings. The books Brecht had read, and the books I had read, praised the kings for the fantastic cities they'd built, the fantastic cities with their gates and their towers and their arches. For the writers of books and the readers of books, civilization was great. How fabulous to stand before these wondrous feats of construction and design! But it was a lie to say that the kings built the cities. They didn't build them. And for the peasants and slaves and prisoners of war who actually built them, civilization might not have been great.

As more and more years of my own life followed on and on, I started to be able to see the past in the present, right in front of me, always more clearly—the "story of civilization." The story of civilization was repeated in front of me every day. I'd seen it even in childhood—we all had—the horrors of the playground, the horrors of the schoolyard. The bigger, stronger kid—the kid with the luck to have a little extra strength—could make the weaker kid do what he wanted him to do: The candy bar was handed over, and nothing really could be done about it. We learned the simple lesson: strong triumphs over weak—among lions, among elks, among boys and girls. Men pin women to the ground—and right then they begin to believe that women are inferior—intellectually inferior, humanly inferior. The people with the guns learn that they can easily defeat the people with the spears, and they begin to say that people so easily defeated are "savages," ignorant, and deserve to be slaves.

For the lucky ones on the banks of the Nile, the lucky ones who were right there in the right place at the right time when the river overflowed, it was all fantastic. Fertile land. More could be grown than they even needed—a surplus! How amazing! So, should the surplus be shared with the less lucky people who lived farther from the river and had less fertile soil? No! We won't share it, and in fact we'll use some of it to feed an army to defend us in case anyone doesn't agree with our plan to keep all the surplus for ourselves. And so the lucky people with the surplus passed it all on to their children, their friends, the children of their friends. Once all of that had happened, well, actually exploiting the people who lived farther from the river was almost an after-thought. Let's put them to work. Why shouldn't we? Get them to till the fields, and if they also produce a surplus, we'll take that too. And then, we'll get them to carry on their backs the massive fragments of stone, carry them and push them all the way up, up, to the top of the pyramid—cities, gates, statues, temples, palaces. And we realize that those who are reduced to doing all this agonizing work must obvi-ously be made of inferior clay—if they weren't, they wouldn't have allowed us to do to them what we've done to them. And if we do have more than these sad, pitiful people, if we have an advantage, why shouldn't we use it? Why not leverage our advantage to get still more? Do you have five times more than that other guy? Why not ten times more? Why not a hundred times more? For the lucky people, civilization just got more and more fun.

And the process has never stopped. And so the lucky people either have more—or they have much more—or they have much, much more—because a person can be lucky, or very lucky, or very, very lucky—and of course lucky people can also be rapacious, or they can be very rapacious, or they can be very, very rapacious. And the jobs that lucky people have are different from the jobs that unlucky people have. Lucky people give orders. Unlucky people obey orders. Lucky people may actually love their jobs. Their jobs can be lively, their jobs can be thrilling. When they go to work, lucky people are treated with respect. Because lucky people respect each other, and everyone else respects them too. But many unlucky people aren't treated with respect, because lucky people, if they want to, can treat them with contempt. And even if the lucky people don't want to treat them with contempt, can they really respect them? No, not really. How could they really respect people whom they know they could so easily treat with contempt?

There are lucky countries, too, and unlucky countries. If you're an unlucky person, and you're working in, let's say, the United States, and your supervisor doesn't think you work fast enough, or he thinks you ask to go to the bathroom too frequently, he can yell at you or make you work on the late night shift; if you're an unlucky person, and you're working in, let's say, Bangladesh, and your supervisor doesn't like your attitude, he can hit you; and if you're an unlucky person, and you're working in, let's say, Colombia, and your supervisor thinks you're a rebel or a troublemaker, he can say a word to some local goons, and he can have you killed.

Lucky people tend to expand, to fill the space their luck has given them. In the city where I live, for example, if you go into any expensive restaurant, you'll quickly learn that very lucky people are often very loud. In those expensive restaurants, the very lucky feel at home, they feel free, they talk very loudly, and sometimes their laughter seems to come up so naturally from the very depth of their bodies that every part of their bodies vibrates and resonates, and their exploding laughter fills the whole room. Unlucky people are often silent. If they're slapped, they're silent. If they're punched, they're silent. If they're shot, they're silent. But every once in a while in certain places, certain moments occur in which the lives of the unlucky have become so painful, so intolerable, that they suddenly look at the lucky people in a very different way, a very strange way, and they suddenly become aware that a terrible injustice has been perpetrated on them, and they cry out, a strange sort of cry of anguish and rage. Unexpectedly, abruptly, there are suddenly riots in certain cities. Cars are overturned. Plate-glass windows are shattered. Indentured farmers burn down the mansion of the landlord. Huge bands of people run out of their houses and try to storm the palace of the ruler.

Teachers

In my early years, the very liberal private schools I attended employed quite a number of unusual teachers, teachers whose approach to life might often have seemed to be at cross-purposes with what one might have assumed to be the attitudes of most of the parents whose children were their pupils. The children's fathers were doctors, lawyers, a few were bankers, and most of them had reached those relatively privileged roles in society through steely ambition and competitive struggle. Yet many of these teachers—not all, of course, because we did have a few who were quite old-fashioned—many of these teachers, one would have to say, were rather decadent characters, rather surprising men and women who despised the generally applauded virtues of heroism, manliness, and devotion to "the group." They didn't seem very loyal to any particular team or country, and they didn't seem to approve of the idea that individuals ought to struggle to achieve supremacy. Instead of encouraging competition, they told us quite openly that they didn't believe in it. And the example many of them set us was one of languid self-indulgence and unembarrassed pleasure-seeking. Some of them devoted their lives to art. None of them devoted their lives to making money, and none of them had any.

Civilization

Not long ago I visited some wealthy friends, a young husband and wife who'd employed the same house-keeper for several years. The housekeeper was a warm, friendly, very sensible woman. She took care of the children, did some cleaning and cooking, and I too had known her for quite a while and always called her by her first name. She had worked for the husband before he was married, and when she and the husband chatted and joked together, I could see all the husband's customary tension falling away. He basked in the affection and the intimacy of this relationship they had. It was easy for him, because he knew where he stood; the relationship's terms had been settled long ago. They proceeded from one day to the next on the basis that, after all, he was a superior being, and so, that being the standing assumption, they both behaved in an appropriate style, he with gentle goodwill toward her, she with a kind of amused, informal, joshing deference toward him. And at a certain point during my visit, she knelt down to pick up the toys that the children had left under the dining room table, and I suddenly imagined that she was throwing the toys with all of her might into the husband's face, blinding him, and then that she was smashing his head into the corner of the marble table-top with overpowering force two or three times until he was dead.

Well, such things don't really happen—do they? Of course the housekeeper knows that only bad consequences would follow if she should murder her employer. And of course most of the time she actually believes that he's a superior being, and so there isn't anything objectionable about the simple fact that he has a superior position in the world, and there's no particular reason to think about murdering him. And it does seem to be the case that he is superior. After all, if he weren't superior, why would he be the employer and she the housekeeper? If he weren't superior, why would she be working for him six days a week, doing all the things he asks her to do? If he weren't superior, why wouldn't he occasionally be working for her? Obviously, that never happens. Every day they play the same parts, and even after years, there's never been a single day on which she gave the orders, and he obeyed them, and so it seems awfully clear that he must be superior. And what does he himself think? Well, he's much too refined to say this out loud, but yes, he secretly thinks that he does possess some special hidden merit, something deep inside him that does make him superior, something perhaps reflected in his way of speaking, his accent, the fact that he excelled in certain subjects at school, his ability to work so seriously at his desk—and he has a good idea of how a superior person would walk and dress and behave, and so he acts that way, he actually impersonates a superior being every moment of his waking life. But of course, at the same time, he's well aware that he's a total fake—he's a fraud—an imposter. What can one say? One has to marvel at the amazing ability of the human mind to accept and contain at the same time two entirely contradictory propositions. Because the remarkable fact is that she also is not at all stupid, and she also knows that the game the two of them play every day is completely insane, she also knows that of course he's not really superior, and she's not really inferior, it's just that he's had much, much better luck—he was given some opportunities, and he took advantage of them. She knows he's an imposter—and that's a very scary thought, and she knows she has to try not to think it, because if she actually thought it for too long, she might want to kill him, which is exactly what she doesn't want to do. She knows very well that the way to find happiness in this world is not to hate your life but to somehow learn how to accept your life. Take pride in your work, whatever it is. Derive whatever pleasure you can from whatever surrounds you—the sky, the people you like, the light falling on the brick wall.

Morality

But I've actually lived long enough now to have figured out what the word "morality" really refers to. I do know what it means, although it's pretty outrageous. It refers to a very simple thought: we shouldn't accept this principle that strong inevitably triumphs over weak. Luck has distributed strength in an arbitrary way: this lion is stronger, this elk is stronger, this group of people lives closer to the river, this group of people lives farther away. Luck has given the person with the penis, the people with the guns, a bit more strength, and so they've trampled over everyone else. Morality says we shouldn't accept that. For the bigger kid to take the smaller kid's candy bar is not right; it's wrong. And if the bigger kid gives that candy bar to me, the process by which I received it was wrong, and it's wrong for me to have it, and it's wrong for me to eat it.

A Cry

Today a cry of anguish and rage is rising into the air from some of the followers of the religion of Islam. And we're totally shocked! It was surprising enough when strangely dressed religious leaders took over the government of such a large country as Iran. But now, these bin Ladenists!? The tactics they've used are bloodthirsty, sadistic. They shamelessly show their pleasure when their enemies are killed. They touch their victims, they look at their faces. They film the killings! These are all things that we would never do—well, except on very rare occasions, like the time when we killed bin Laden himself. And the reasons they give for their anger seem odd, because their language is religious. A rather large number of people in the West could understand—and many could respect, and quite a few could even deeply admire—the Marxist rebels in Southeast Asia or Latin America who fought so bravely against the ruthless dictators and elites installed in power by the United States. Those who rebel today under the bin Ladenist flag are much, much harder to sympathize with.

But we need to remember that the Western powers, with their enormous fleets of airplanes and ships, have over the decades and centuries forced into a degrading subjugation virtually all the lands where Islam is practiced and immense Islamic empires once ruled. Places whose political, economic, and intellectual influence had once reached across the globe have been forced to submit to the military might of foreign conquerors, and dignified people have been compelled to stand by helplessly as their lands were demeaningly carved into pieces and given new names by alien overlords. And we should accept

the fact that, even though Osama bin Laden happened to have been rich, the bin Ladenist movement
is a movement of the poor. Almost all of his followers, and the followers of his followers, have been very
poor and very unlucky people, just like the followers
of the Marxist revolutionaries, and the movement
would not exist at all if it didn't express the desperation of these particular people. Some of the members and supporters of the bin Ladenist movement
are middle-class or upper-class individuals, just as
there have always been middle-class and upper-class
participants in virtually all movements of the poor,
because there have always been certain members of
the privileged classes who, for whatever reason (in
Osama bin Laden's case, perhaps partly because his
family was recently poor), have sympathized with,
and identified with, very poor people.

To eat bad food when you know that others eat
good food, to not have food, to be responsible for
children and not be able to feed them well, to be sick
and know that other people can see a doctor, but

you and your family have no doctor you can see, to live surrounded by dirt, to live in ugly rooms in ugly buildings, to know that you can easily be robbed of everything you have, to live in fear of being beaten up, to live in fear of being raped, to live in fear that you or your loved ones could be hurt or killed by people whose authority you cannot challenge—well, yes, poverty is a filthy condition. And when desperate people cry out and risk their lives to say that their condition is awful, they're basically never wrong. They may be wrong about what caused their condition, they may be wrong about what will cure their condition, but people who do terrible things because they're in a state of desperation about the circumstances they live in are not deluded. The boy at the party in the hotel ballroom thought his problem was that there was another boy who was flirting with his date. That wasn't his problem. His problem was bad schools, bad health, bad prenatal care, bad childhood nutrition, danger, terror, daily harassment, condescension expressed by authorities who underestimated his intelligence, the fact that in the building he lived in, the garbage was collected on an irregular schedule, the elevator was broken, the light bulbs in the hallways and the stairwells were broken. The boy's action, the murder, was a form of speech; he was trying to say something.

But, of course, we're puzzled or sometimes almost incredulous when followers of Islam are rioting in the streets or even occasionally killing people because of what we might see as one or another not terribly egregious insult to their religion: in a prison located thousands of miles away from them, a copy of the Koran has been thrown onto the ground, or kicked, or burned. But when people have no control over their own lives, and no feeling of safety, and they don't know how to find the few basic things they need in order to survive, it's not surprising that they hold on tight to their religion—it may be the only thing they have left, and they're afraid that even that might somehow be taken away from them. We can't be surprised by the fact that they adore their religion.

Religion can mean solace and serenity, a kind of security, a private small garden of kindness in a desert of cruelty that seems to stretch out as far as they can see. For people who love the book, for whom the Koran is the fountain that provides the world's only goodness, an insult to the book can feel more painful than blows that are inflicted on their own bodies.

A Storm

And then a couple of decades after our visit to East Berlin, it was an autumn evening, and we were about to have dinner in our lovely apartment, which has large windows looking out on a broad street a couple of blocks away from a very large river. There was a big storm outside, some noisy rain, and all of a sudden the lights in our apartment went out. We'd been through a couple of brief urban blackouts in recent decades, and they always seemed a bit funny, as if we were living in some distant village on a mountaintop, and so we brought out some particularly nice candles and lit them, and I stood in the kitchen in a rather cheerful mood as some sausages quietly fried on the stove, and then we heard weird sounds, a loud honking of cars, and we ran back to our windows and saw something impossible—it was the large river coming down the street, effortlessly crashing into people's basements and pouring inside. And at first I was fascinated and exhilarated by the power of the storm, the magnificence of nature breaking out of its bounds. But by the next morning, when I began to realize that the electricity was not going to be quickly coming back on, and there would be no running water and no heat coming up the pipes, and no one was going to come over and fix things for us, I experienced a feeling of disorientation, as if a lifetime's worth of assumptions were uncontrollably unspooling, and I began to fall into a bizarre state of depression that was unprecedented for me. My sense of humor dropped down, down, all the way to zero. I sat on the bed for hours in the darkness, not moving, not being able to believe how low I had sunk in such a short time as the temperature inside continued to drop.

By the time I had lived long enough to seriously understand what had been explained to me about civilization in that small apartment so many years before, by the time I had seen enough examples of the "story of civilization"—the endlessly repeating story of a strong person holding some squirming weak person's head under the water—seen it enough to really get the message—the vast machinery of civilization itself seemed to be stretching, weakening, and pulling apart . . .

Bin Ladenists

In an incomprehensible development that caused confused hurt feelings among people in the West, many young Muslims living in the slums of British and European cities were beginning to experience what one could possibly call the pain of the amputated limbs of the Islamic world. These young people had been born in the West but were living with parents and grandparents who had grown up in colonized countries as colonial subjects. Now grandparents, parents, and children were all trying to make a life in the lands of the former colonizers, and it wasn't easy. The young people had to take on the burden of the complex emotions of their parents and grandparents, the conscious anger built up over a lifetime and the unconscious anger built up over a lifetime, as well as dealing with their own personal struggles, and at the same time they were constantly watching images on television and the Internet of the countries their families had come from, and the people whose images they were looking at were constantly being blown to pieces all over again by Western invaders. And rather magically or uncannily, many of these young British and European Muslims found that they were suddenly feeling, as if it were their own, the suffering of fellow Muslims in Gaza or Iraq or Syria or Afghanistan, and, seized by a desire to finally put an end to the era of Islamic humiliation at the hands of the West, a few of these young people actually wanted to fly to the Middle East and join the bin Ladenists. This caused audible murmurs in the councils of the lucky, who apparently had no sooner overcome the challenge to their position posed by the atheistic voices of the revolutionary Marxists than they found themselves challenged once again from a different direction by the religious voices of the bin Ladenists.

In England, the Conservative prime minister David Cameron threw himself with abandon into a passionate struggle over young Muslim brains. This earnest man, who was not himself a believer in Islam, and who may or may not have known a lot about Islam, and who—well—quite possibly couldn't have cared less about Islam or any possible interpretation of Islam, nonetheless desperately hoped to find teachers of Islam whose interpretation of the Islamic texts would coincide properly with his own ideas about how Muslims in Britain ought to feel and behave. His benign hope that young Muslims would come to be inspired by a Cameron-friendly type of Islam was then backed up by a program of monitoring, in which ordinary teachers of mathematics or English in British schools were required to make reports to higher authorities if indications appeared that any of the brains in their classrooms were starting to mutate in the wrong direction.

I recalled the one very puritanical teacher I'd had at my school when I was eleven or twelve—her classroom was right next door to the classroom of an elderly woman who was rumored to be a nudist on weekends—and this puritanical teacher was very concerned that we, her pupils, thought too much about sex and had even brought to school certain magazines about sex that contained nude pictures, and so she tried to interest us in different magazines that dealt with what people at that time called "current events"—"international affairs," what was happening in the world. But in David Cameron's classrooms, the teachers became concerned if the students started thinking too little about sex. The teachers were on notice that if students started to dress more conservatively or behave more decorously, if they lost interest in gossiping and started to pray more frequently, if they stopped going to parties and began to read magazines about international affairs, then the higher officials at their schools had to be quietly notified. More importantly, if the children started to believe that Britain and the United States had invaded Iraq in 2003, or that hundreds of thousands of Iraqis had died as a result, then they became potential candidates for thought-retraining programs in which they could relearn how to forget that these things had happened, or relearn how not to care that they had happened, or relearn how not to be upset that they had happened. And if the children began to feel that as Muslims they were looked down upon and discriminated against, that politicians were making hostile statements about them, that their employment prospects were poor, or that they lived in slums, then law enforcement had to be quietly alerted, names taken down, and more serious surveillance seriously considered.

Across the English Channel, a more openly antireligious campaign is still in progress, because many French politicians and many French intellectuals (still at war, as it seems that they are, with the Catholic Church) seem to be not at all shy about denouncing religion itself—religion in general and Islam in particular. As everyone knows, French lawmakers have promulgated the remarkable rule that young Muslim women are not allowed to wear headscarves in school. In other words, if they want an education, young Muslim women are obliged to violate what some of them consider an important tenet of their faith, and they're obliged to appear in public dressed in a way that many of them see as unacceptably immodest, as if Christian girls had to go to school topless. One recent French commentary on bin Ladenist violence in France suggested that the French themselves ought properly to be blamed for it, because French people, according to the commentary, have refused to speak out in their daily lives against the Islamic religion and its various customs. If a Muslim happened to own the sandwich shop on the corner, and the Muslim shop owner declined to sell sandwiches containing pork—this was one example given—then, in the opinion of this commentary, the non-Muslim customer who had wanted such a sandwich ought to openly complain to the shop owner about the ridiculous characteristics of the Islamic religion, rather than meekly looking for his ham sandwich in a different shop. This same attitude of refusing to be sensitive to other people's religious beliefs has led some French intellectuals to defend or even applaud the famous Danish cartoons depicting and mocking Muhammad, along with various similar French cartoons, even though many Muslims believe that the image of the Prophet should not be drawn at all, and even though it clearly causes pain to a large group of individuals to see the person they love and revere being treated disrespectfully, particularly when the disrespect shown to the Prophet runs parallel in their own lives to the disrespect shown every day toward them.

Although it might seem to be clear that what the world needs at the moment is more sensitivity, rather than less, and what French Muslims need is less humiliation, rather than more, the doggedly enthusiastic French proponents of mockery and their various supporters in other Western countries, whenever they're asked what benefit their joking brings to the planet, repeatedly speak of the universal right to freedom of speech and claim that those who dislike their brand of humor want to restrict people's right to say what they like—to which it could certainly in turn be objected that to defend everyone's right to say what they like may be quite appropriate but doesn't remotely require anyone to have any respect or regard or admiration at all for all the vicious, unkind, cruel, horrible, and disgusting things that certain people enjoy saying to hurt other people—and that certain other people enjoy saying to disparage unpopular non-majority groups—denigrating such groups being a delightful, historically popular sport, known to have an important role in the creation of social prejudice, hate, pogroms, lynchings, and genocide.

Officials of the US government, of course, have a simpler, two-point solution to the problem of bin Ladenism—point one being, if you see any bin Ladenists living nearby in your own country, lock them up and throw away the key; point two being, in any country that can't prevent you from doing it, kill all the bin Ladenists using bombs and drones.

But the truth is that none of these various approaches to fighting bin Ladenism will actually work. The British approach of trying to indoctrinate and monitor furiously angry people in the hope that they'll adopt a moderate view of life won't work. The French approach of denouncing people's religious beliefs or forcing them to violate some of their religious principles won't work. And the American approach of putting people into prison or killing them most certainly won't work. People who already feel intolerably restricted will only grow angrier when placed in prisons, and the policy of going to different countries and trying to kill all the bin Ladenists, whether by bombing them in large numbers or by firing specialized missiles at them in small groups or one by one, has mysteriously encouraged the growth of bin Ladenism in country after country, because virtually all the bin Ladenists being killed on the ground (not to mention the children, neighbors, and others being killed because they were too close by when the bomb went off) are desperate, poor, very unlucky people, and when the world's most insanely rich and luckiest people start to send bombs into the villages, homes, schools, hospitals, funerals, and wedding parties of people who already are and always have been horribly unlucky, this is so nauseating that great numbers of other unlucky people—those nearby and even those far away from all over the world—will rush to stand by the side of the unlucky victims.

The truth is that once unlucky people come to understand how unlucky they are, it's too late for the lucky. That knowledge cannot be unlearned. Once the right of the lucky to dominate the world has been questioned, the lucky are in trouble. The weird specter of "right" and "wrong" has risen up off the ground and can't be contained.

As long as the world is divided into two groups, those who are lucky and exploit others, and those who are unlucky and are exploited by the lucky, there will always come a moment in one place or another when one of the unlucky people is going to say, "Wait—this is wrong." Of course human beings are articulate creatures, so people who are angry are going to find words to express their anger, whether those words are Marxist words, bin Ladenist words, or any other sort of words. Admittedly, it would be hard to deny that the lucky in the West had quite a lot of success in trying to wipe Marxist words and Marxist ideas off the face of the earth by using the technique of killing Marxists. Indeed, you could make the case that in certain places in the world, unlucky people turned to religious teachers for inspiration and guidance precisely because so many of those who provided inspiration and guidance from a Marxist perspective were dead. You could even say that because of the killing of Marxists by the Western powers, there are places in the world in which the thoughtful, compassionate ideas of Marx were directly replaced by the cruel, reductive ideas of Osama bin Laden. But the unavoidable reality is that even if all the Marxists and all the bin Ladenists were to be safely dead, and all the words they used were to be completely forgotten, so long as the subjugation of unlucky people continued, new words would be found. The feeling of "right and wrong" seems to be somehow innate; it's un-expungeable.

Inspiring and noble groups and individuals have fought against the oppression of the unlucky, and there have also been groups and individuals who were involved in the same struggle who were not inspiring. The bin Ladenists are not inspiring; perhaps they are a manifestation of a sort of frustration or despair that's unusual even among organized groups of tormented people. All the same, one has to recognize that they represent the flamboyant edge, at this particular moment, of the same movement that Marx joined in the nineteenth century and that traces its mostly unwritten history back to the day the first exhausted and broken worker carrying massive fragments of stone up a pyramid turned to a fellow worker and quietly asked the question, "Is there any way to get out of this?"

It's a question that could be asked at any moment by many billions of people who live on our planet.

Upheaval

It's a dreadful fact that the hard labor of unlucky people has so often brought them little benefit, and that so many in effect have devoted their entire lives to increasing the wealth and glory of their lucky employers. Of course unlucky individuals have always had the power to withhold their labor and stop the machine, or even to break the machine and kill the owners of the machine, although the price people have paid for doing such things has often been death. Two things in particular, though, mean that a serious upheaval, a change from "below," a change led by the unlucky, a change in how the world is organized, is more possible now than it has been before. The first is that worldwide communication between unlucky people is now possible. The second is that dramatic change of some kind is inevitable anyway, because either some sort of rationally controlled global change will somehow occur, or chaotic change will soon come about, because the rivers are flowing down city streets, and most of the living species on earth, including ours, will one by one begin to sicken and die.

If things go well, the life of the unlucky might improve. No matter what happens, the life of the lucky is going to change.

Of course, if we think that the life of the lucky will change, then we might be curious about who belongs to the group of the "lucky." Certainly we're all aware of the famous group of very, very rapacious people who are the best known and most successful subset of the group of people who are very, very lucky, and those would be the millionaires and the billionaires who are reasonably called the "1 percent." But I'd say "the lucky" are a larger group. Roughly speaking, I'd say that if your city has not been bombed, if your loved ones have not been raped, tortured, or killed, if you've never been harassed or beaten by the police, if you're not afraid to walk after dark on the street where you live, if you have a place to live in which you're not unbearably cold in the winter or unbearably hot in the summer, if you eat two or three fairly healthy meals a day, and if you're not regularly shouted at or threatened or punished by your boss or his managers at work, then you probably count as a lucky person, and so that would include, for example, a very large number of the citizens of the United States and Great Britain and most European countries. Those citizens are plausibly to be counted among the lucky because, whether they know it or not, their relatively comfortable lives are made possible by the twist of luck that arranged for them to be born into fortunate positions in prosperous countries, and the prosperity of their countries derives in very large part from the

unjust exploitation of various unlucky human beings, some still living and some now dead.

The United States, for example, has been engaged since 1945 in an extraordinarily audacious
attempt to use its military and economic power
to dominate, control, or manipulate the behavior
of basically every country on earth; it's an attempt
that obviously has had good years and bad years
but that on the whole has been surprisingly successful. The purpose of this amazing project has
simply been to preserve an international status
quo, an international balance of power, which al-
lows a lot of Americans to remain rich. Many individual Americans have opposed some of the
more brutal and horrible regimes that their government has succeeded in imposing on certain
unlucky nations, and they have spoken, written,
and marched in opposition to many of the wars
and campaigns of the US government, and they
have voted against political candidates whose
policies they found particularly heartless and

militaristic. Nonetheless, even these dissenting individuals have probably benefited personally, in their material lives, from the great prosperity of their country, which would not exist were it not for the powerful international position of the United States. Certain particular policies of the US government have undoubtedly been self-defeating and in their own terms counterproductive and have served to weaken rather than strengthen the position of the United States, but it would be foolish for any American to declare with any degree of certainty—if the clothes they're wearing are comfortable and clean, if they can travel to a different city or a different country on a family vacation, if they can go to the movies or eat in restaurants—that the brutal policies of the United States, financed by the taxes they've paid, have not played a role in allowing them to enjoy those comforts. And of course the exploitation that brings prosperity to the prosperous goes very far back into the past as well. The people of Great

Britain and Europe are still benefiting today from the exploitation of colonized peoples in the nineteenth century, and the people who live in the United States today are still benefiting from the exploitation of nineteenth-century enslaved people in the South whose unpaid labor made possible the creation in the North of the American industrial cornucopia—and also from the deaths of the many millions of Native Americans who once walked and slept and cooked and thought on the very spots where US citizens now go to buy espresso machines, or reenact battles, or ski.

Obviously, no one can prove that a just world in which no one was subjugated and no one was oppressed would be a peaceful world in which no one would be tempted to murder his neighbor, and in which cruel practices and cruel ideologies would simply disappear, and the human race would reverse course and begin to devote itself to protecting the planet and all living creatures. But clearly if we simply keep going the way we're going now, a horrible death, for the rich as well as for the poor, surely can't be escaped. We need to find a path to a better world. Our only hope is to find that path.

We need a better world right away, this week. An upheaval is desirable—perhaps it's inevitable. And yet we've learned some things about ourselves over the last hundred years, and that knowledge makes a difference. We can't ignore the things we've learned. If, as a species, we start to find our way, through effort and imagination, toward a different sort of world, certain individuals and groups will find themselves taking the first steps, and one has to hope that they will keep what we've learned very much in mind. And the most important thing we've learned is that we don't understand ourselves.

We have to remember the murderer in the courtroom who said, "I don't know." We have to recognize that no matter who we are, even if we happen to be among the very few people who can honestly claim to have spent their whole lives struggling to create a better and more just world, all the same, we are human beings, and we don't know ourselves. We don't understand ourselves. But we do know for sure that other people and all living things need to be protected from us, because we're very dangerous. We may be unknowable, and it would be insane to trust us.

Even if what we want is a better life for everyone, we have to remember what species we belong to, and we have to watch ourselves very, very carefully.

Taking pleasure in triumphing over others, taking pleasure in having control over others, taking pleasure in telling others what to do, taking pleasure in the suffering of others, taking pleasure in being the cause of the suffering of others, taking pleasure in the death of others, and then, the extra thirty-seven blows that words can't seem to explain—what response can we have when this creature approaches?

Self-deception, too, we've learned, is a thunderingly powerful force in human affairs. No one can hide from it. No one is exempt from it. The ability to believe, falsely, that we know our own motives and that those motives are good, is an affliction that can befall those whose motives were once indeed good just as easily as it can befall those whose motives have always been bad. And just as the possession of wealth or a high status in society makes a person's engine of self-deception race faster, so too does the possession of power over others, and so too does the use of physical violence.

It seems undeniable that once it begins, violence leads us into some sort of madness, some terrifying maze inside the mind in which we become lost, and we don't know what's happening or what we ourselves are doing. In 1945, a group of us dropped an atomic bomb on the city of Hiroshima. Various people gave explanations for that. And then three days later, we dropped another atomic bomb on Nagasaki. Were there explanations for that as well? It doesn't matter. It really doesn't matter. I'm saying that the means of violence should not be entrusted to members of the human race. Power over the lives of other human beings should not be entrusted to members of the human race. I think that the long scientific experiment has given us some very clear results by now: humans are not equipped to handle these things.

Most of those who have dreamed of a more just world, who have perhaps spent their lives trying to prepare for one, have confronted the cold intransigence of the world's entrenched elites, the dug-in repositories of luck and strength, and they've come to the conclusion that these ruthlessly greedy and heartless people will never give up power if blood is not spilled, that only violence can possibly dislodge them. And yet those who triumph in violent combat are by definition triumphant; they're by definition victors, and they're by definition powerful, and, whatever else they are, at that moment of victory they're strong, and they're lucky. At least at that moment, they've become the lucky elite.

And this brings us naturally to the questions of revenge and punishment. Because if the unlucky were ever indeed to remove the lucky from their current position of supremacy, the issue of "what to do about the lucky" would immediately be on the table, and the questions of revenge and punishment would immediately arise.

We all, naturally, dream of revenge. It's one of the most enjoyable and thrilling of fantasies. We all become excited when we imagine the day when those whom we've learned to despise, those whom we feel have gotten away with so much for so long, will finally pay a price, will finally receive the reward they've earned. And yet—the person who takes revenge, at that very moment, becomes too powerful; the person who punishes, at that very moment, becomes too powerful.

Revenge and punishment both imply, "Even if I'd been you, and I'd had your life, I would never have done what you did." And that in turn implies, "I wouldn't have done it, because I'm better than you." But the person who says, "I'm better than you" is taking a serious step in a very dangerous direction. And the person who says, "Even if I'd had your life, I would never have done what you did" is very probably wrong.

There is a thing inside each of us that we experience as the will, the "I." We're all aware that there are warring impulses inside us, and sometimes we feel that our will is on one side and some powerful internal force is on the other side. Some people struggle not to drink alcohol. There's an institute in Sweden that helps principled people who find themselves struggling with a sexual attraction to children. In privileged societies, many people struggle with themselves not to eat the extra rolls that remain sitting on the table when the dinner is over. We all go through various sorts of struggles, and sometimes the thing we experience as our "I" wins, and sometimes it loses. What we don't know, though, and what science can't tell us, is whether it was ever possible for that struggle to have had a different outcome from the one it had. In my opinion, and I can't prove that I'm right, though I can't be proved wrong, the answer is probably never yes.

If two people compete in a game of tennis, no one knows who will win before the game begins. But when the game is over, it's often possible for a skilled observer to explain why the winner won. The outcome was ultimately determined by the way that the strengths and the weaknesses of the two players interacted in that particular game on that particular day in that particular place. Struggles that take place inside a human being are harder to observe, but I've never seen any reason to doubt that the facts about a person's current circumstances, in addition to the facts about their current personal makeup— their original genetic composition, changed and developed by the habits and beliefs and psychological characteristics they've acquired during their lives— determine the outcome of their inner struggles. The struggle inside the human being is very real, just as the tennis game is real. Before the tennis game begins, no one knows what factors will influence it. No one knows, for example, that a sudden noise will distract one of the players at a crucial moment.

All the same, the sum of the factors—including the sudden noise—will determine the outcome of the game. And in a similar way, the balance of forces within the individual—including their reactions to the environment around them—will determine the outcome of their inner struggles. If an alcoholic tries not to drink and fails, it's because their impulse to drink was too strong, or their will was too weak, or both were true, and in any case, their "I" "lost control" over their actions—that is, they did what their "I" truly didn't want to do. Did they struggle as hard as they could? We can't know whether they did or not. Did they create their own nature and determine how strong their will would be? No, they didn't.

I can decide that I want to become a better person. I can try to become a better person, and maybe I'll succeed. But I don't have the ability to discard all the elements of myself that may make that task of becoming a better person difficult.

When danger suddenly appears in our lives, and we need to make a choice—allow the escaped slave, hunted Jew, or undocumented refugee to hide in our house or send them away—we might turn out to be courageous, or we might turn out to be cowardly. In that moment of crisis, a vast number of factors that are hidden from our own consciousness are set feverishly to work inside us. Our fear of the price we might have to pay for a courageous choice is a factor, but so are the things our various friends and loved ones have said to us over the years, so are the books we may have read, so are the examples set by people we know and people we don't know. In the first moment of crisis, we have no idea what we're going to do. But to tell our friends today that if a crisis comes tomorrow, we know we'll be courageous, is simply foolish. And to righteously denounce the person who ultimately made the cowardly choice is foolish also. "Morality" may—if we're fortunate—tell us what the better choice is and help us to fight for it within ourselves. Morality can influence our behavior; perhaps in some cases it will determine our behavior. But the actual process of decision-making takes place in secrecy; it happens in a private room from which we're escorted out at the last moment. And even if we know what the right choice is, and we long to make that choice, the balance of forces inside us may compel us to go in the opposite direction.

Bernard Madoff was an intelligent and successful New York business executive who swindled a great many people out of an extraordinary amount of money. Radovan Karadžić was a Bosnian Serb psychiatrist and politician who committed many war crimes during the 1990s Bosnian war, including ordering the deaths of eight thousand people who had gone to an area called Srebrenica that the United Nations had declared to be a safe zone. Did Madoff have the ability not to swindle his clients? Did Karadžić have the ability not to massacre the people in Srebrenica? And what about me? If I'd been in their circumstances, would I have done the things they did? Possibly not, if I were still me. But if I had had Madoff's brain and Madoff's life, I would have been Madoff, and I think I would have done what Madoff did, and if I'd had Karadžić's brain and had had Karadžić's life, I would have been Karadžić, and I think I would have done what Karadžić did. And consequently I can't help feeling that the whole apparatus of blame, judging, hatred toward those who've done terrible things is fundamentally wrong and ought to be discarded, and that punishment and revenge are based on assumptions that are fundamentally false.

Punishment, of course, is one of the possible techniques a community can use (a time-honored one, obviously) to indicate or emphasize what sort of behavior it doesn't like or doesn't condone, and the fear of punishment can certainly influence people's behavior. And in certain cases perhaps people find it actually enjoyable to exact revenge. All the same, punishment and revenge are both still unjust, because there's absolutely no way to determine that the person being punished, or the person against whom revenge is taken, was capable of behaving differently from the way they behaved.

Through no fault of their own, most unlucky people are born into bad circumstances from which no amount of ingenuity will allow them to escape. But also through no fault of their own, most lucky people are born into good circumstances, from which they may or may not want to escape but from which in any case they rarely do escape. Most of these lucky people lack the originality or the boldness or the imagination that would be required in order for them to give up their pleasant life and devote themselves to the welfare of humanity. And most are never provided with the intellectual tools they would need in order to see through the worship of greed and the self that the influential figures in their privileged environment are eager to teach them, and so they become greedy and selfish people. So let's try not to be hypocrites. Let's recognize that we all are born with a great number of capacities inside us, and then, well, life has its way with us. Certain of our capacities are activated, and others are not, and we turn out one way or another.

Some of us turn out to be brave, generous, and kind. Others turn out to be not particularly wonderful people. But there's no good reason to condemn, revile, punish, or kill the lucky, the privileged, or the greedy. If some of them are awful people, or if from a certain point of view they're all awful, they became awful through the same ordinary human process that applies to everybody.

We don't yet know how that human process works. What enables us to do good things or terrible things? Even among nations, the mechanism remains opaque. After World War II, Germans quite rightly asked themselves, How could we have done what we did? They examined their culture, their child-raising practices, even their language, endlessly trying to comprehend, Why are we worse than other people? In the years since World War II, though, it's been the jovial, friendly Americans, with a completely different culture, different child-raising practices, and a different language, who were responsible for ghastly activities in Vietnam, Latin

America, Iraq, and a great many other places, while the Germans, retaining the same language they had before, along with much of the same culture and certain of the same child-raising practices, have kept themselves very low down on the list of post-war international killers. Casting one's mind back to days gone by, there are reasons to say that the Belgians are actually the worst people, but one could mention also the English, or the French. The honor of being the worst seems to travel strangely between nations, which means that each nation in itself is not intrinsically either demonic or not demonic, though of course the Germans were horrifying in a German style, and the Americans are horrifying in an American style.

It's our desperate task to figure out what, exactly, activates this capacity for unspeakable behavior that we all possess. Those who hope to create a better world particularly need to brood about that question, because of the particular dangers they themselves might present if their struggle to change the existing order should manage to succeed. Success is dangerous. It's a lot like luck.

Teachers
The teachers in the fascinating schools I attended were subversively guiding us toward the "downward mobility" that some of us later experienced. They were quietly leading us away from our society's obsession with self, power, prestige, and money. Perhaps, they imagined, it might be possible for some of us, or all of us, to develop a character that was less grasping, more yielding. Very slyly, they were giving us a hint that we might just possibly want to slip away altogether from the elite world of the lucky into which we'd been born. And I must have been listening to what those teachers were saying because not many years later I became deeply involved in a love affair with someone whose apartment was extremely small, with poorly installed plumbing—and whose feeling about the apartment was that it wasn't really that bad.

I myself still haven't escaped the desire for comfort. I like comfort, I like comfort enormously—even luxury, if I can get my hands on it. But my teachers softened me up, without any question. I'd say I'm halfway to decadence. My manliness gauge stands at more than half empty. And that's also true for many of my friends. And many of their friends. If someone says to me, "Your air conditioner uses energy sources that are raising the level of carbon dioxide in the atmosphere," I may take a hard look at the person who's saying it, think for a moment, and ignore what they said. But if all my friends gave up their air conditioning units, I wouldn't insist on keeping mine. And if some day next week or some day a few years from now, the great masses of the unlucky should come to my door and want to confiscate my air conditioner or even my entire apartment, I'm pretty sure that I won't fight them. I'm pretty sure I'll simply give up. I'll simply surrender. If some of my neighbors form an army of the lucky to fight the unlucky, I won't join. I'm much too lazy to fight for what I have, and what would make me an impossibly poor soldier in the army of the lucky is that I don't really believe I have a right to what I have. I know that my side is not the right side. I know that my life has always been wrong. So today I can very easily live my life and enjoy my life, even love my life, but if the moment comes, I won't kill for it, and I won't even fight for it.

In other words, I'm saying that one way that a great upheaval could possibly occur without the shedding of blood would be if those who are now the lucky elite could already, today, be privately at work on quietly melting and softening their own shells, to use a snail metaphor, so that ultimately they would all become small worm-like creatures who wouldn't fight and couldn't fight. And this is not a preposterous fantasy. The children of the most ruthless executives and military commanders very often turn out to be delicate aesthetes who want nothing more than to play with puppets or make long necklaces out of small colored beads.

Civilization

The people who wrote the books with which Brecht quarreled didn't consider the possibility that civilization might have been a mistake. If they'd been asked about it, they probably would have agreed with the frighteningly thin man who believed that Beethoven's music, being the end product of a process that saw humans go from hunting and gathering to being members of modern society, was a sort of infallible indicator that the process itself was purely admirable. If we confront Beethoven's music, they would probably have argued, we are confronting something that's undeniably good, and so the development of civilization, which led to Beethoven, can never be regretted. But this ignores the suffering that accompanied civilization. Because suffering is also a kind of absolute. When we see photographs of the fire in the sweatshop, when we see the pictures of the parents grieving over their daughters who worked in the sweatshop, we are face to face with what is undeniably not good.

If one were seriously to consider this odd question—was civilization a mistake?—of course one would need to speculate about the happiness or unhappiness of the hunter-gatherers who came before civilization—which is notoriously difficult to do—and one would need to guess whether the life of a hunter-gatherer in the Africa of many millennia ago was a better life than the life of a sweatshop worker in Africa today. And of course, in brooding about the question of civilization, one does have to note that the worst consequences of civilization may not have occurred yet; they may be just around the corner. And one also has to note that we can't quite reach a verdict on civilization at the present moment, because it's at least theoretically possible that we might still be able to change course, to go in a different direction, and so we can't be sure that civilization won't eventually be twisted inside-out into a shape that will be enormously beneficial. In any case, civilization is what we have now, and so—short of a horrifying cataclysm—electricity, cities, books, poetry, mathematics, physics, paintings, and quartets will be the sorts of things we have at our disposal to work with if a better world is ever to be made.

To get from where we are now to some less terrifying place will be, if not completely impossible, certainly way beyond difficult, and so it almost goes without saying that the human beings who might carry out such an extraordinary creative task need to be as inspired and insightful and intelligent and deep as members of the species can possibly be. And here is where we must say that civilization itself could come in handy, because some of the things that civilization has learned how to do could prove amazingly useful in the struggle to save the world from some of the things that civilization is now doing. Because civilization has actually figured out how to store up and preserve human wisdom from over the millennia and has devised remarkable methods for refining and sharpening the individual human mind.

Civilization has come up with many precious objects that can cause the human mind to expand, but many of these objects have been hoarded in the locked treasure rooms of a tiny number of individuals. And many of the treasures have fallen victim to a fate that is common to things that are kept in locked rooms; no one quite remembers where they are, and after a while they're completely forgotten. We need to break into those rooms, because we need all the help we can possibly get.

There's no reason to doubt that every healthy human infant is born with the potential to play music beautifully, to read with sensitivity, to do scientific research, to put on plays, to draw and paint, and certainly to think. To think, to understand, to reason, to analyze arguments. And naturally also, to develop, to grow. But almost all of those who are born unlucky have been brutally prevented from developing more than a fraction of their own abilities, and this is perhaps the most shocking fact about our human world.

Undoubtedly less shocking, but possibly more weird, is the incredible fact that in the contemporary world many even of those who are born lucky are voluntarily forgoing the opportunity to develop their inner resources. Gorgeous and delicious fruits, grown by seductive geniuses, sit on the plates of these lucky people but remain uneaten. A process of decay has infected the lucky in various parts of the world, and very notably in the United States, leading many even of the luckiest to turn vehemently against complex thought in general and the cultivation of the intellect in particular—and even to turn against complex pleasures. And in certain circles, crude thought and ignorance are openly respected and praised, while the concept of basing one's conclusions on carefully gathered information (or on replicable experiments)—and even the principle of rationality itself—are ignored or even mocked. Traveling in precisely the opposite of the direction that would help the world to dig itself out of its crisis, many lucky people have come to believe that our spiritual and mental lives should have only two elements: first, everyone should learn whatever technical skills are necessary in order for them to be able to work and make money (skills learned by the unlucky would bring them a small amount of money, skills learned by the lucky would bring them a large amount of money) and second, for relaxation, people should consume very simple pleasures such as very simple stories, very simple music, very simple eroticism, and various sadistic forms of amusement such as television programs that show people insulting or tormenting each other or killing each other. Omitted from this short list of recommended intellectual activities—and from the type of education that can be derived from it—is anything conducive to the development of the wide-awake, thoughtful, curious, sharply logical, and deeply emotional human beings who could save the world, on the one hand, or, if a better world were to be created, could actually enjoy it. And regrettably, the human beings whose mental life would conform to the plan these individuals consider desirable would be ill equipped intellectually to defend themselves against manipulation and control by cunning supporters of the status quo and all the glittering species of egomaniacs with whom we're all too familiar.

In other words, the expansion of every individual's potential would be what we would hope would happen in a better world, but if it doesn't happen to some extent in the world we're in now, we're never going to get to anything better.

The Lucky

If anyone is reading this, there may be members of the group of the lucky among them, and to them I would simply say, Yes, it is highly unlikely that a better world will come about, but if by some miracle it does, it may be better for you than you think it will be. Of course it will be difficult to break your habits and addictions, though, obviously, it will be somewhat easier for your children to break theirs. But if the time comes, you're going to be able to learn how to live without your car and your coffee-bean grinder. You could eventually get used to a life in which you didn't give orders. You could even get used to doing your share of the irreducible minimum of unpleasant labor that happens to be necessary to maintain the processes of life on which we all now depend. Vegetables must be grown in the countryside, and there are parts of the process of farming that can't be done by machines and that no one likes to do, and, in the cities, people have to crawl down under the streets to maintain the sewers, and in a more just world, the work that absolutely no one wants to do would probably have to be shared, with every able-bodied person doing some of it each week or each month, and so one of the people who'd be doing it would sometimes be you, and after a while you'd be quite all right with that. And yes, you'd have to live in a smaller apartment. Maybe a much, much smaller apartment, but if all went well, you'd still be able to read, cook, and play music, and after a while you might come to feel that it really wasn't that bad.

Night

Night is a wonderful blessing. It's amazing, and I'm so grateful for it. In the darkness, lying in bed, we can stop. To be able to stop—that's amazing. We can stop. We can think. Of course it's frightening too. We think of what may happen to us. We think about death. Murders and murderers stand around the bed. But night gives us a chance to consider the possibility that we can start again, that when day comes we can begin again in a different way.

The aggressiveness that has been our daily mode of being can't help us any more. We wake up and start massacring people whom we see as our enemies. We wake up and break into the earth with gigantic drills and terrifying explosions. We wake up and find our place in a monstrous final struggle. On the one side, there are all the lucky people, and on the other side, strangely allied together, we find all the unlucky people, plus the birds, the crickets, the ladybugs, the bees, the monkeys, the parrots, the forests, and the rivers. At the moment, the lucky people are clearly winning, and almost all the evidence seems to indicate that they'll ultimately prevail. The nonhuman creatures and the unlucky people are running from place to place, gassed, strafed, shot at, booby-trapped, gasping for breath. And the living planet that we've blasted and bombed and injected with poison is now, like an enormous animal who's been tortured for hours by some horribly disturbed demented children, finally beginning to die, and its terrible groans are dreadful to hear. But the animal may not die, if we can convince the children, who are ourselves, to stop killing it. It's perhaps still a possibility that we might be able to stop being murderers. This could be our night, and during this night we might be able to stop. Stop. Think. And start again in a different way.

ACKNOWLEDGMENTS

To publicly name the people who kindly offered thoughts on the manuscript of this "essay" might expose them to ridicule, so I won't do that, but I am enormously grateful to I, D, D, C, B, and A, you know who you are—and, *natürlich*, D.

ABOUT THE AUTHOR

Wallace Shawn is an Obie Award–winning playwright and a noted stage and screen actor. His plays *The Designated Mourner* and *Marie and Bruce* have been produced as films, as has his translation of Henrik Ibsen's *The Master Builder.* He is co-author of the movie *My Dinner with Andre* and the author of the plays *The Fever, The Designated Mourner, Aunt Dan and Lemon,* and *Grasses of a Thousand*

Colors, as well as the nonfiction books *Essays* and *Night Thoughts* (Haymarket Books). His latest play, *Evening at the Talk House,* premiered at the Socialism conference in Chicago and was performed at The National Theatre in London and The New Group in New York. His plays *Designated Mourner* and *Grasses of a Thousand Colors* will soon be available as multipart podcasts.

About Haymarket Books

Haymarket Books is a radical, independent, nonprofit book publisher based in Chicago. Our mission is to publish books that contribute to struggles for social and economic justice. We strive to make our books a vibrant and organic part of social movements and the education and development of a critical, engaged, international left.

We take inspiration and courage from our namesakes, the Haymarket Martyrs, who gave their lives fighting for a better world. Their 1886 struggle for the eight-hour day—which gave us May Day, the international workers' holiday—reminds workers around the world that ordinary people can organize and struggle for their own liberation. For more information and to shop our complete catalog of titles, visit us online at www.haymarketbooks.org.

Also Available from Haymarket Books

Freedom Is a Constant Struggle: Ferguson, Palestine, and the Foundations of a Movement
Angela Y. Davis

Hope in the Dark: Untold Histories, Wild Possibilities
Rebecca Solnit